D1349182

VEGETARIAN COOKING

HAMLYN

COOK'S NOTES

OVEN TEMPERATURES

°C	°F	GAS MARK	
70 C	150 F	Low	–
80 C	175 F	Low	–
90 C	190 F	Low	–
100 C	200 F	$\frac{1}{4}$	–
110 C	225 F	$\frac{1}{4}$	Very slow
130 C	250 F	$\frac{1}{2}$	Very slow
150 C	275 F	1	Slow
160 C	300 F	2	Moderately slow
170 C	325 F	3	Moderately slow
180 C	350 F	4	Moderate
190 C	375 F	5	Moderately hot
200 C	400 F	6	Hot
220 C	425 F	7	Hot
230 C	450 F	8	Very hot
240 C	475 F	9	Very hot

MICROWAVE POWER SETTINGS

Power Level	Percentage	Numerical Setting
HIGH	100%	9
MEDIUM HIGH	75%	7
MEDIUM	50%	5
DEFROST	30%	3
LOW	10%	1

SOLID WEIGHT CONVERSIONS

METRIC	IMPERIAL
15 g	$\frac{1}{2}$ oz
25 g	1 oz
50 g	2 oz
100 g	4 oz/$\frac{1}{4}$ lb
175 g	6 oz
225 g	8 oz/$\frac{1}{2}$ lb
350 g	12 oz
450 g	1 lb
575 g	1$\frac{1}{4}$ lb
700 g	1$\frac{1}{2}$ lb
800 g	1$\frac{3}{4}$ lb
900 g	2 lb

MICROWAVE

Microwave tips have been tested using a 650 watt microwave oven. Add 15 seconds per minute for 600 watt ovens and reduce the timings by 5-10 seconds per minute for 700 watt ovens.

LIQUID VOLUME CONVERSIONS

METRIC	IMPERIAL
25 ml	1 fl oz
50 ml	2 fl oz
125 ml	4 fl oz
150 ml	5 fl oz/$\frac{1}{4}$ pt
175 ml	6 fl oz
225 ml	8 fl oz
300 ml	10 fl oz/$\frac{1}{2}$ pt
450 ml	15 fl oz/$\frac{3}{4}$ pt
600 ml	20 fl oz/1pt
900 ml	1$\frac{1}{2}$ pt
1.2 l	2 pt
1.7 l	3 pt

AUSTRALIAN CUP CONVERSIONS

	METRIC	IMP
1 cup flour	150 g	5 oz
1 cup sugar, granulated	225 g	8 oz
1 cup sugar, caster	225 g	8 oz
1 cup sugar, icing	175 g	6 oz
1 cup sugar, soft brown	175 g	6 oz
1 cup butter	225 g	8 oz
1 cup honey, treacle	350 g	12 oz
1 cup fresh breadcrumbs	50 g	2 oz
1 cup uncooked rice	200 g	7 oz
1 cup dried fruit	175 g	6 oz
1 cup chopped nuts	100 g	4 oz
1 cup desiccated coconut	75 g	3 oz
1 cup liquid	250 ml	9 floz

WEIGHTS AND MEASURES

Metric and Imperial weights and measures are given throughout. Don't switch from one to the other within a recipe as they are not interchangeable. 1 tsp is the equivalent of a 5 ml spoon and 1 tbls equals a 15 ml spoon.
All spoon measurements are level, all flour plain, all sugar granulated and all eggs medium unless otherwise stated.

SYMBOLS

 FREEZER TIP

 SERVING SUGGESTION

 MICRO-WAVE TIP

 WINE & DRINK NOTE

CONTENTS

STARTERS	**4**
SIDE DISHES	**18**
MAIN COURSES	**26**
BASIC RECIPES	**62**
INDEX	**64**

First published in Great Britain 1993
by Hamlyn
an imprint of Reed Consumer Books Limited
Michelin House, 81 Fulham Road, London SW3 6RB
and Auckland, Melbourne, Singapore and Toronto

ISBN 0 600 57771 6

A CIP catalogue for this book is available at the British Library

All rights reserved. No part of this publication may be reproduced, stored in a
retrieval system, or transmitted in any form or by any means,
electronic, mechanical, photocopying, recording or otherwise, without the prior
permission of the publisher.

Produced by Mandarin Offset
Printed and Bound in Singapore

MIXED VEGETABLE MOUSSES

Peter Reilly

With their three colourful layers of puréed vegetables and glossy yellow pepper sauce, these mousses look as good as they taste.

PREPARATION TIME: 30 MINS
COOKING TIME: 1 ½-2 HOURS
SERVES 4

I N G R E D I E N T S

225 G/8 OZ CARROTS, CHOPPED

225 G/8 OZ SWEDE, DICED

SALT AND GROUND BLACK PEPPER

225 G/8 OZ BROCCOLI FLORETS

2 EGGS, BEATEN

3 TBLS DOUBLE CREAM

GRATED ZEST OF 2 ORANGES

BUTTER, FOR GREASING

¼ TSP GROUND NUTMEG

8 SLICES MELBA TOAST,
TO SERVE

CHERVIL LEAVES, TO GARNISH

FOR THE PEPPER SAUCE

2 YELLOW PEPPERS, SEEDED AND
SLICED

1 SMALL ONION, FINELY CHOPPED

2 TBLS OLIVE OIL

125 ML/4 FL OZ VEGETABLE STOCK

4 TBLS DOUBLE CREAM

4 Preheat the oven to 180 C/350 F/ Gas 4. Grease 4 ramekins or individual oval moulds. In each ramekin, put enough carrot purée to fill one-third of the dish. Tap the base gently on the work surface to level the mixture. Then spoon in the swede purée so that the ramekin is two-thirds full. Tap to even the mixture. Fill evenly to the top with broccoli purée.

5 Put the ramekins in a roasting tin with water to come half way up the sides and cover with buttered foil. Cook for 1-1½ hours until the mousse is firm to the touch and slightly coming away from the sides.

1 Put the carrots and swede in a saucepan of salted cold water. Cover and bring to the boil. Put the broccoli in a steamer and place it on top of the carrot and swede saucepan. Cover and cook for 20-25 minutes until all the vegetables are tender. Alternatively, boil the broccoli in a separate pan for 5 minutes or until tender.

2 Drain all the vegetables well, and put each one in a separate bowl. Purée each vegetable separately starting with swede, then the carrot and lastly the broccoli.

3 Stir 2 tbls egg, 1 tbls double cream and one-third of the orange zest into each bowl of purée and season with salt and pepper and nutmeg.

6 To make the pepper sauce: soften peppers and onion in the oil in a covered saucepan for 5 minutes. Add the stock, bring to the boil and simmer for 10 minutes. Cool slightly, then process until smooth. Return the sauce to the pan. Add the cream and heat through. Turn out the vegetable moulds and serve with the sauce and garnish.

ROQUEFORT & LEEK TARTLETS

Peter Reilly

The piquant taste of Roquefort combines with juicy leeks to make these moreish little tarts.

PREPARATION TIME: 15 MINS
COOKING TIME: 30 MINS
SERVES 4

I N G R E D I E N T S

225 G/8 OZ SHORTCRUST PASTRY, (SEE RECIPE PAGE 62)
1 EGG YOLK, BEATEN
25 G/1 OZ BUTTER
2 LEEKS, TRIMMED AND FINELY SLICED
75 G/3 OZ ROQUEFORT CHEESE
FRESH CHOPPED PARSLEY, TO GARNISH
FOR THE SAUCE
15 G/½ OZ BUTTER
15 G/½ OZ FLOUR
150 ML/¼ PT MILK
150 ML/¼ PT SINGLE CREAM
2 TBLS CHOPPED FRESH PARSLEY
SALT AND GROUND BLACK PEPPER

3 To make the sauce, melt the butter in a saucepan. Stir in the flour and cook over a gentle heat for about 30 seconds. Remove from the heat and gradually stir in the milk. Add the cream, chopped parsley and season to taste. Return to a gentle heat and stir continuously until thickened.

4 Divide the leeks between the pastry cases and spoon the sauce over the leeks. Crumble the Roquefort cheese on top and set them under a hot grill until golden brown. Sprinkle with chopped parsley.

1 Preheat the oven to 200 C/400 F/ Gas 6. Roll out the pastry and use it to line 4 individual fluted tartlet cases. Brush the pastry with beaten egg and prick the base all over using a fork. Bake for 15-20 minutes. Keep warm.

2 Meanwhile, melt the butter in a frying-pan and sauté the leeks until they are tender. Cover and set aside until ready to use.

TIP

SET THE TARTLET CASES ON A BAKING TRAY WHEN REMOVING AND RETURNING THEM TO THE OVEN. THIS PREVENTS ANY DAMAGE BEING DONE.

SERVE THE TARTLETS WITH BABY CARROTS, NEW POTA-TOES AND FRENCH BEANS.

WILD MUSHROOMS IN BASIL SAUCE

Peter Reilly

Exotic, creamy and simple to prepare, these mushrooms in basil sauce melt in the mouth.

PREPARATION TIME: 10 MINS
COOKING TIME: 10 MINS
SERVES 4

I N G R E D I E N T S

8 SLICES OF WHOLEMEAL BREAD

125 G/5 OZ BUTTER

2 TBLS FINELY CHOPPED FRESH
PARSLEY

3 SHALLOTS, FINELY CHOPPED

450 G/1 LB WILD MUSHROOMS SUCH
AS CEPS, CHANTERELLES, FIELD
MUSHROOMS, SLICED IF NECESSARY

300 ML/½ PT SINGLE CREAM

150 ML/¼ PT DOUBLE CREAM

5 TBLS THINLY SHREDDED BASIL

SALT AND GROUND WHITE PEPPER

FRESH BASIL LEAVES, TO GARNISH

2 Heat 50 g/2 oz of the butter in a frying-pan and fry the bread on both sides until it is golden. Remove and set aside. Brush edges of bread with 25 g/1 oz melted butter and coat with finely chopped parsley.

1 Using a 9 cm/3½ in round fluted cutter, stamp out 1 round from each of the bread slices.

3 Wipe out the frying-pan and melt the remaining butter. Fry the shallots until softened and then add the mushrooms. Stir and cook for 2-3 minutes. Add both the creams, chopped basil and seasoning to the pan. Bring to the boil and simmer until slightly reduced and saucy. Arrange the toasts on serving plates and divide the mushrooms in sauce between them. Garnish with fresh basil leaves and serve.

WATCHPOINT

ONLY USE FRESH BASIL IN THIS RECIPE.
DRIED BASIL DOES NOT HAVE SUCH A
DELICATE FLAVOUR.

LAYERED VEGETABLE TERRINE

Peter Reilly

Colourful, unusual and a vegetarian's delight, this terrine is easy to prepare.

PREPARATION TIME: 25 MINS

COOKING TIME: 1 ½-1 ¾ HOURS

SERVES 4-6

I N G R E D I E N T S

175 G/6 OZ WHOLE CABBAGE LEAVES

700 G/1 LB 8 OZ CAULIFLOWER
FLORETS

225 ML/8 FL OZ DOUBLE CREAM

2 EGGS, BEATEN

SALT AND GROUND BLACK PEPPER

2 TSP MEDIUM CURRY POWDER

100 G/4 OZ THIN CARROTS

100 G/4 OZ SMALL COURGETTES,
HALVED LENGTHWAYS

1 RED PEPPER, SEEDED AND CUT
INTO 2.5 CM/1 IN STRIPS

2 STICKS OF CELERY, STRINGS
REMOVED

OIL, FOR GREASING

A SELECTION OF SALAD LEAVES, TO
SERVE

Lightly oil a 900 g/2 lb loaf tin and line
it evenly with the blanched cabbage
leaves, overlapping them to leave no gaps,
and allowing enough leaves to overhang
the edges of the tin.

4 Put a layer of cauliflower purée in
the tin to a depth of 12 mm/½ in.
Lay the courgettes lengthways on
the purée, then cover with more purée.
Continue layering with the carrots, celery,
pepper strips with the cauliflower purée,
and finally, finishing with a layer of purée.
Fold the cabbage leaves to enclose the top
of the terrine. Cover the tin loosely with a
piece of oiled foil.

1 Preheat the oven to 190 C/375 F/
Gas 5. Blanch the cabbage leaves
for 2-3 minutes, plunge into cold
water. Drain. Remove stalks.

2 Boil the cauliflower for 15
minutes. Drain. Purée with the
cream, eggs, salt, pepper, and
curry powder. Set the mixture aside.

5 Sit the terrine in a bain-marie and
bake for 1¼-1½ hours. Remove
the tin and allow it to stand for 10
minutes. Remove the foil and carefully
turn the terrine onto a warm serving dish.
Serve it cut in thick slices with a leaf salad.

3 Boil the other vegetables for 5-10
minutes, or until tender. Drain
thoroughly. Skin pepper strips.

TIP

IF YOU LIKE YOUR FOOD HOT AND SPICY,
YOU CAN USE A CURRY POWDER THAT IS A
LITTLE STRONGER.

LEEK TERRINE

Michael Michaels

A cool vegetarian terrine complemented by
feta cheese, walnuts and a hint of lime.

PREPARATION TIME: 25 MINS
+ CHILLING
COOKING TIME: 10 MINS
SERVES 6

I N G R E D I E N T S

| 15 LEEKS, CLEANED |
| SALT AND GROUND BLACK PEPPER |
| 175 G/6 OZ FETA CHEESE |
| 75 G/3 OZ WALNUT HALVES |
| 50 ML/2 FL OZ SALAD OIL |
| 3 TBLS WALNUT OIL |
| JUICE OF 1 LIME |
| LIME SLICES, TO GARNISH |

3 Pack the leeks lengthways into the loaf tin or terrine. Arrange the layers of cooked leeks head to tail. Lay over a piece of baking parchment.

4 Fit a piece of stiff card into the loaf tin on the parchment, and weigh it down well with two tins of food. Leave overnight in the fridge.

1 Trim the dark green part from the leeks, slice them lengthways and cut them to fit a 900 g/2 lb loaf tin or terrine lengthways.

2 Boil the leeks in salted water until tender – slightly more than al dente but not enough to spoil the bright green colour. Dunk them in cold water to cool as rapidly as possible, then drain and dry thoroughly on a clean cloth.

5 Next day turn the leek mould out and with a very sharp knife slice across into 6 thick slices.

TIP

THE LEEK SLICES MAY FALL APART, BUT WITH CARE THEY CAN BE REASSEMBLED ON EACH DINER'S PLATE. A RAZOR SHARP KNIFE OR ELECTRIC CARVING KNIFE IS A MUST HOWEVER.

6 To serve, garnish each slice with a little Feta cheese and walnuts. Mix together the oils and lime juice, and season well with salt and ground black pepper. Spoon it over the leek terrine. Garnish with the lime slices.

CREAM STUFFED KOHLRABI

Michael Michaels

Turnip-flavoured kohlrabi is at its best served with a creamy filling.

PREPARATION TIME: 15 MINS
COOKING TIME: 1-1¼ HOURS
SERVES 4

I N G R E D I E N T S

4 KOHLRABI, TRIMMED

1 TBLS VEGETABLE OIL, PLUS EXTRA
FOR GREASING

1 ONION, FINELY CHOPPED

1 STICK OF CELERY, CHOPPED

1 TBLS CHOPPED DILL

SALT AND GROUND BLACK PEPPER

25 G/1 OZ BREAD, DICED

150 ML/¼ PT SOURED CREAM

SPRIGS OF DILL, TO GARNISH

LIME WEDGES, TO GARNISH

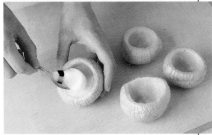

3 Remove the woody tops from the kohlrabi and discard. Carefully hollow out the flesh using a spoon, leaving the walls about 6 mm/¼ in thick.

4 Chop up the flesh and add to the vegetables in the pan. Add the diced bread along with the soured cream. Give it a stir to coat with cream and heat gently for 1 minute.

1 Preheat the oven to 180 C/350 F/ Gas 4. Put the kohlrabi on an oiled baking tray and cook in the oven for 45-50 minutes.

5 Spoon the filling into the kohlrabi shells and return to the baking tray. Bake for a further 10-15 minutes or until heated through. Put on serving dishes and garnish each kohlrabi with sprigs of dill and a couple of wedges of lime, before serving hot.

2 Heat the oil in a large frying-pan, add the onion, celery, dill and seasoning. Cook until soft. Remove from heat and set aside.

SOUFFLE AVOCADOS

Peter Reilly

Try avocados hot in a light-as-air soufflé with
a parmesan and sesame seed topping.

PREPARATION TIME: 20 MINS
COOKING TIME: 16-21 MINS
SERVES 6

I N G R E D I E N T S

50 G/2 OZ BUTTER, PLUS MELTED
BUTTER FOR GREASING

50 G/2 OZ FLOUR

300 ML/½ PT MILK

¼ TSP CAYENNE PEPPER

DASH OF TABASCO

50 G/2 OZ PARMESAN CHEESE,
FINELY GRATED

SALT AND GROUND BLACK PEPPER

2 SMALL AVOCADOS

4 LARGE EGGS, SEPARATED

15 G/½ OZ FRESH BREADCRUMBS

15 G/½ OZ SESAME SEEDS

heat and gradually beat in the milk.
Return to the heat and slowly bring to the
boil, stirring all the time. Remove from the
heat and stir in the cayenne pepper,
Tabasco, 40 g/1½ oz of the Parmesan
cheese and salt and pepper.

3 Halve the avocados, then remove
the stone and skin. Mash the flesh
until smooth. Stir in the cheese
mixture, then add the egg yolks.

4 Whisk the egg whites in a large
bowl until they form stiff peaks but
are not too dry. Carefully fold the
egg whites into the avocado and cheese
mixture until it is just combined. Divide
mixture between the dishes to fill. Run the
blade of a small knife around the inner
wall of each dish – this will help the
soufflés rise evenly.

1 Preheat the oven to 200 C/400 F/
Gas 6. Brush six ovenproof
avocado dishes with butter.

5 Mix together the breadcrumbs,
remaining Parmesan and sesame
seeds and sprinkle over the tops of
the soufflés. Put the dishes on a baking
tray. Bake for 15-20 minutes.

2 Melt the butter in a small
saucepan, add the flour and cook
gently for 1 minute. Take off the

STUFFED TOMATOES

Michael Michaels

Garlic flavoured pasta makes an appetising
filling for sweet beef tomatoes.

PREPARATION TIME: 20 MINS
COOKING TIME: 40 MINS
SERVES 6

INGREDIENTS

6 LARGE BEEF TOMATOES

450 ML/3/4 PT TOMATO SAUCE
(SEE RECIPE PAGE 62)

2 TSP SUGAR

1 TSP FINELY CHOPPED FRESH
MARJORAM

75 G/3 OZ BUTTER

1 LARGE SPANISH ONION, ROUGHLY
CHOPPED

1 CLOVE OF GARLIC, CRUSHED

450 G/1 LB WHOLEWHEAT PASTA
SHELLS OR TWISTS

150 ML/¼ PT SOURED CREAM, TO
SERVE

3 Cook the pasta in boiling salted water until just tender (al dente). Drain well and rinse with boiling water, then add the cooked onions and garlic. Mix together so that the onion and butter evenly coats the pasta.

4 Stuff the tomatoes with the pasta and onion mixture. Put the tomato lids back on and put in an ovenproof dish. Pour in the tomato sauce and bake for 20 minutes. Give each guest a stuffed tomato, a spoonful of sauce, and hand the soured cream around separately as an optional extra.

1 Preheat the oven to 200 C/400 F/ Gas 6. Cut a thick slice off the tops of the tomatoes, keeping the lids intact. Scoop out all the pith, juice and seeds and place in a bowl. Push the mixture through a sieve and add to the tomato sauce with the sugar and the chopped fresh marjoram. Simmer over a gentle heat until thick and pulpy.

2 Melt the butter and slowly cook the onion until it is soft and transparent, but not coloured. Add the crushed garlic and cook the mixture for a further 30 seconds.

CELERIAC GRATIN

Michael Michaels

Sliced celeriac is covered in a Cheddar-based sauce and grilled for that golden finish.

PREPARATION TIME: 10 MINS
COOKING TIME: 20 MINS
SERVES 4

INGREDIENTS

700 G/1 LB 8 OZ CELERIAC, PEELED
1 TBLS VEGETABLE OIL, PLUS EXTRA FOR GREASING
4 SPRING ONIONS, TRIMMED AND CHOPPED
2 TBLS FLOUR
300 ML/½ PT MILK, WARMED
25 G/1 OZ CHEDDAR CHEESE, GRATED
1 TSP GRATED NUTMEG
SALT AND GROUND BLACK PEPPER
2 TBLS PARMESAN CHEESE, GRATED
1 TSP CAYENNE PEPPER

3 Heat the vegetable oil in a frying-pan and add the chopped spring onions and sauté for 2 minutes. Sprinkle in the flour and cook for 1 minute. Stir in the milk.

4 Bring the sauce to the boil, stirring all the time. Add the grated Cheddar, nutmeg and seasoning.

1 Cut the celeriac into 6 mm/¼ in slices and put them in a pan of boiling water. Boil for 10-15 minutes or until they are just cooked. Drain the slices well.

2 Lay the celeriac slices in a lightly greased ovenproof gratin dish, so that they overlap each other a little.

5 Pour the sauce over the celeriac. Sprinkle the Parmesan cheese and cayenne pepper on top. Set under a preheated grill and grill until the top turns golden.

BRAISED CHICORY WITH APPLE

Clint Brown

Here, the slightly bitter taste of chicory is softened by the addition of sweet red apples.

PREPARATION TIME: 10 MINS
COOKING TIME: 15 MINS
SERVES 4

INGREDIENTS

450 G/1 LB CHICORY

2 SMALL RED APPLES

JUICE OF 1 LEMON

1 TBLS VEGETABLE OIL

SALT AND GROUND BLACK PEPPER

2 TBLS CIDER VINEGAR

1 Cut the chicory into 2.5 cm/1 in slices. Then quarter and core the red apples and cut them into 1.2 cm/½ in thick slices.

2 Put the slices of chicory and apple, the lemon juice, vegetable oil and seasoning into a large saucepan. Add 150 ml/¼ pt water to the pan. Then cover and bring to the boil. Reduce the heat to a gentle simmer.

3 Poach the chicory and apple until it is tender, for about 5 minutes. Remove the lid and pour in the cider vinegar and stir well. Allow some of the liquid to evaporate.

4 Reduce the heat and cook until the chicory and apple are softened, about 5 minutes. Transfer to a serving dish and serve hot.

TIP

RASPBERRY VINEGAR IS A PLEASANT ALTERNATIVE TO CIDER VINEGAR.

RATATOUILLE

Alan Newnham

Serve this wonderful fusion of courgettes,
aubergines, tomatoes and peppers steaming
hot, or chilled with a dash of orange juice.

PREPARATION TIME: 40 MINS
COOKING TIME: 25-30 MINS
SERVES 4-6

I N G R E D I E N T S

1 AUBERGINE, SLICED
SALT
2 TBLS OIL
1 ONION, SLICED
2 COURGETTES, THICKLY SLICED
1 GREEN PEPPER, SLICED
1 RED PEPPER, SLICED
1-2 CLOVES OF GARLIC, CRUSHED
1 TBLS FRESH PARSLEY, CHOPPED
400 G/14 OZ TINNED TOMATOES, CHOPPED
GROUND BLACK PEPPER

Diana Miller

3 Finally add the parsley and tomatoes and season with pepper. Leave to simmer for 15-20 minutes before serving.

m COOK THE SLICED AUBER-GINES, ONION AND 2 TBLS OIL AT HIGH (100%) FOR 3 MINUTES IN A MICROWAVE-PROOF DISH. ADD THE COURGETTES, PEPPERS AND GARLIC AND COOK FOR 2 MINUTES, ADD THE PARSLEY AND TOMATOES AND COOK FOR 6-7 MINUTES, STIRRING TWICE. SEASON AND SERVE.

1 Put the aubergine slices on a plate and sprinkle with salt. Leave to drain for 20 minutes, then rinse thoroughly in cold water. Pat dry with kitchen paper. Heat the oil in a saucepan and sauté the aubergine and onion until the onion becomes almost clear. Aubergines absorb a lot of oil when they are being cooked, so you may find that more oil is needed to stop the vegetables catching on the base of the pan.

2 Add the courgettes, peppers and garlic and fry for another 5 minutes, stirring occasionally, and adding more oil if necessary.

TAGLIATELLE WITH MUSHROOM SAUCE

Peter Reilly

Thick mushroom sauce piled on top of tagliatelle makes this a substantial meal with a real Italian flavour.

PREPARATION TIME: 10 MINS
COOKING TIME: 10 MINS
SERVES 4

I N G R E D I E N T S

450 G/1 LB GREEN AND RED
TAGLIATELLE

50 G/2 OZ BUTTER

50 G/2 OZ FLOUR

600 ML/1 PT WARM MILK

4 TBLS MUSHROOM KETCHUP

SALT AND GROUND BLACK PEPPER

225 G/8 OZ MASCARPONE

225 G/8 OZ MIXED MUSHROOMS,
SLICED

FLAT-LEAVED PARSLEY, TO GARNISH

and seasoning. Remove from the heat and blend in the Mascarpone.

3 Add the sliced mushrooms to the sauce and simmer slowly for 4 minutes until the mushrooms are soft. Bring to the boil making sure you stir the sauce all the time.

1 Put the green and red tagliatelle in a pan full of boiling water. Cook for 4 minutes.

4 Arrange the tagliatelle on a serving plate. Pour over the creamy mushroom sauce and garnish with flat-leaved parsley.

TIP

TRY A COMBINATION OF MUSHROOMS SUCH AS OYSTER, CHESTNUT AND BUTTON MUSHROOMS IN THE SAUCE.

2 Melt the butter in a saucepan, add the flour and cook for a minute. Gradually add the milk, stirring continuously. Add the mushroom ketchup

PEPPER TOMATO SAUCE WITH PASTA

Clint Brown

A colourful blend of vegetables in a tasty tomato sauce served with pasta quills makes a delicious vegetarian main course. Serve with a sprinkling of Parmesan cheese.

PREPARATION TIME: 15 MINS
COOKING TIME: 25 MINS
SERVES 4

INGREDIENTS

2 TBLS SUNFLOWER OIL

1 ONION, SLICED

1 CLOVE OF GARLIC, CRUSHED

3 PEPPERS — RED, YELLOW AND
GREEN, DICED

2 COURGETTES, SLICED

100 G/4 OZ MUSHROOMS, SLICED

2 STICKS OF CELERY, SLICED

400 G/14 OZ TINNED TOMATOES

1 TBLS TOMATO PUREE

2 TBLS RED WINE

1 TBLS CORNFLOUR

300 ML/½ PT VEGETABLE STOCK

2 TSP OREGANO

2 BAY LEAVES

SALT AND GROUND BLACK PEPPER

350 G/12 OZ PASTA QUILLS

25 G/1 OZ BUTTER

2 Blend the cornflour with the stock and add to the vegetables along with the herbs. Bring to the boil, stirring until thickened. Season to taste. Cover and simmer for 20 minutes.

3 Meanwhile, bring a pan of salted water to the boil, add the pasta and cook for 10 minutes. Drain, toss in butter and serve immediately with the sauce.

 COOK VEGETABLES AND OIL IN A MICROWAVE-PROOF BOWL ON HIGH (100%) FOR 5 MINUTES. BLEND CORNFLOUR WITH WINE, AND ADD ALL THE REMAINING SAUCE INGRE-DIENTS. COOK ON HIGH (100%) FOR 15 MINUTES, STIRRING TWICE. SERVE WITH THE PASTA.

1 Heat the oil in saucepan and sauté vegetables for 5 minutes, stirring occasionally. Add the tinned tomatoes, tomato purée and red wine.

 TRY THIS SAUCE AS A DELI-CIOUS FILLING FOR BAKED JACKET POTATOES.

SAFFRON PASTA WITH PIMIENTOS

Clint Brown

Saffron may be expensive, but you only need a little. Here it brightens up tagliatelle and contrasts well with red pimiento sauce.

PREPARATION TIME: 10 MINS
COOKING TIME: 12-15 MINS
SERVES 4

I N G R E D I E N T S

350 G/12 OZ TAGLIATELLE

PINCH OF SAFFRON STRANDS

2 TBLS OLIVE OIL

1 SMALL ONION, CHOPPED

1 CLOVE OF GARLIC, CRUSHED

25 G/1 OZ BUTTER

25 G/1 OZ FLOUR

400 G/14 OZ TINNED CHOPPED
TOMATOES

375 G/13 OZ TINNED PIMIENTOS,
DRAINED AND CHOPPED INTO SMALL
PIECES

300 ML/½ PT DOUBLE CREAM

3 TBLS TOMATO PUREE

SALT AND GROUND BLACK PEPPER

GRATED PARMESAN CHEESE,
TO GARNISH

FEW SPRIGS OF FRESH PARSLEY,
TO GARNISH

1 Cook the tagliatelle in a saucepan of boiling water along with the saffron strands and 1 tbls of the oil for 12-15 minutes until it is tender but still firm to the bite.

2 Meanwhile sauté the onion and the crushed garlic in the butter and the remaining oil for 2-3 minutes.

Sprinkle in the flour and cook, stirring constantly, for a further minute before adding the chopped tomatoes and pimientos. Bring the mixture to the boil.

3 Take off the heat and stir in the cream and tomato purée. Heat the sauce gently and when just below boiling point remove from the heat. Sieve or liquidise the sauce then season.

4 Strain the tagliatelle and transfer onto serving plates. Spoon a helping of the pimiento sauce over each plate of pasta. Sprinkle on a little Parmesan cheese and garnish with a sprig of parsley to serve.

A GLASS OF WHITE ITALIAN WINE SUCH AS FRASCATI CLASSICO OR ORVIETO SECCO COMPLEMENTS THIS PASTA.

VEGETABLE CROUSTADE

Clint Brown

This croustade – a hollowed-out round loaf baked to crispy perfection – can be filled with any combination of seasonal vegetables.

PREPARATION TIME: 30 MINS

COOKING TIME: 40 MINS

SERVES 6

INGREDIENTS

1 ROUND LOAF, ABOUT 25-30 CM/ 10-12 IN IN DIAMETER
OIL, FOR BRUSHING
100 G/4 OZ BABY SWEETCORN
100 G/4 OZ FRENCH BEANS
100 G/4 OZ MANGETOUT
100 G/4 OZ CARROTS
1 RED PEPPER
1 GREEN PEPPER
1 YELLOW PEPPER
SALT
½ ONION, CHOPPED
3 TBLS WHITE WINE VINEGAR
3 TBLS VEGETABLE STOCK OR WATER
2 TBLS SOY SAUCE
175 G/6 OZ COLD BUTTER, DICED

1 Preheat the oven to 220 C/425 F/ Gas 7. Cut the top off the loaf, so it is about 7.5 cm/3 in deep. Hollow out the middle, leaving the wall about 2 cm/¾ in thick.

2 Place the loaf on a baking tray and bake for 5 minutes. Brush inside and out with oil, turn upside-down and brush the base with more oil. Bake for a further 10 minutes. Brush all over again with oil and bake for a final 5-10 minutes or until crisp.

3 Meanwhile, prepare the vegetables so they are about the same size as the sweetcorn. Top and tail the French beans and mangetout, then cut the carrots and different coloured peppers into strips. Boil in salted water for 5 minutes then drain.

4 For the sauce: put the onion, white wine vinegar and stock or water in a saucepan and reduce over a high heat until only 1 tbls liquid remains – this will take about 3 minutes. Strain and pour back into the pan. Stir in the soy sauce.

5 Over gentle heat, gradually whisk the butter into the sauce, piece by piece. Whisk until all the butter has been incorporated and the sauce is rich and smooth.

6 Tip the cooked vegetables into the sauce and reheat gently. Using a slotted spatula, remove the vegetables from the pan and pile into the hollow croustade shell. Cut the croustade into wedges and serve with the remaining sauce, poured into a sauce boat.

SWEET & SOUR VEGETABLES

Chris King

Sweet & Sour Vegetables can be served as a
side dish or as a main course for a
vegetarian supper.

PREPARATION TIME: 15 MINS
COOKING TIME: 10 MINS
SERVES 4-6

INGREDIENTS

250 G/9 OZ EGG NOODLES

SALT

2 TBLS SESAME SEED OIL

1 RED PEPPER

1 GREEN PEPPER

2 TBLS SUNFLOWER OIL

225 G/8 OZ TINNED WATER
CHESTNUTS, HALVED

BUNCH SPRING ONIONS, TRIMMED

225 G/8 OZ TINNED BAMBOO
SHOOTS, DRAINED

425 G/15 OZ TINNED BABY
SWEETCORN, DRAINED

FOR THE SAUCE

225 G/8 OZ PINEAPPLE CHUNKS,
DRAINED WITH JUICE RESERVED

2 TBLS VINEGAR

3 TBLS BROWN SUGAR

½ TSP SALT

1 TBLS TOMATO PUREE

1 TBLS SOY SAUCE

1 TBLS CORNFLOUR

2 Remove the seeds from the peppers then cut into diamond shapes. Prepare the sauce: mix the pineapple juice with the vinegar, sugar, salt, tomato purée, soy sauce and cornflour.

Peter Reilly

1 Cook the noodles in a large saucepan of salted boiling water for 2 minutes. Drain and rinse with boiling water to remove excess starch then return to the saucepan. Pour the sesame seed oil over the noodles and toss. Cover the saucepan and keep warm.

WATCHPOINT

BABY SWEETCORN ARE ALSO AVAILABLE FRESH FROM MAJOR SUPERMARKETS AND FROM SPECIALITY SHOPS. COOK ALL THE VEGETABLES FOR 3-4 MINUTES AFTER ADDING THE SAUCE, OR UNTIL THE CORN IS TENDER-CRISP.

3 Heat the wok, add the sunflower oil and heat for a few seconds. Add the peppers, water chestnuts, spring onions, bamboo shoots and sweetcorn and stir-fry for 3 minutes. Pour the sauce over the vegetables, add the pineapple chunks and cook for a further 2 minutes, or until the sauce heats up and thickens.

4 Transfer the cooked noodles to a warmed serving dish, pour the stir-fried vegetables onto them and serve immediately.

CHINESE VEGETABLE STIR-FRY

Alan Newnham

One of the best ways to begin experimenting with Chinese cooking is with this quick and satisfying stir-fry recipe. This can be used as a base for more adventurous dishes.

PREPARATION TIME: 20 MINS
COOKING TIME: 10 MINS
SERVES 4

INGREDIENTS

2 TBLS SESAME OIL
2 CARROTS, SLICED INTO 2.5 CM/ 1 IN SLICES
150 G/6 OZ WHOLE BABY CORN
1 RED PEPPER, SLICED INTO THIN STRIPS
1 GREEN PEPPER, SLICED INTO THIN STRIPS
150 G/6 OZ MANGETOUT, SLICED DIAGONALLY INTO 2.5 CM/ 1 IN PIECES
6 SPRING ONIONS, SLICED DIAGONALLY
150 G/6 OZ BEANSPROUTS
225 G/8 OZ PINEAPPLE CHUNKS IN JUICE
FOR THE SAUCE
2 TSP CORNFLOUR
2 TBLS WHITE WINE VINEGAR
2 TBLS DARK SOY SAUCE
2 TBLS DARK SOFT BROWN SUGAR
SALT AND GROUND BLACK PEPPER
125 ML/4 FL OZ PINEAPPLE JUICE

heat. Heat the oil and stir-fry the carrots and sweetcorn for 2-3 minutes

2 Add the peppers, mangetout and spring onions. Stir-fry for 3 minutes. Add the beansprouts and pineapple chunks and stir-fry for a further minute. Reserve pineapple juice.

3 Slake the cornflour with some pineapple juice and combine with the other sauce ingredients. Pour over the vegetables, stirring all the time until the sauce is thickened and bubbling. Transfer to a warmed serving dish.

1 Have all the vegetables prepared ready for cooking. Heat the wok or large frying-pan over a high

VEGETABLE & CASHEW CURRY

Clint Brown

A mild curry of assorted vegetables with cashew nuts to add texture. If you want to hot it up just increase the amount of spices.

PREPARATION TIME: 30 MINS
COOKING TIME: 35-45 MINS
SERVES 4-6

I N G R E D I E N T S

2 TBLS PEANUT OIL

2 CLOVES OF GARLIC, CRUSHED

¼ TSP GROUND CORIANDER

2 TSP GROUND CUMIN

1 TSP TURMERIC

2 CM/¾ IN FRESH ROOT GINGER,
FINELY CHOPPED

2 POTATOES

2 AUBERGINES, CUT INTO 12 MM/½
IN CUBES

1 SMALL CAULIFLOWER, TRIMMED
AND DIVIDED INTO FLORETS

100 G/4 OZ GREEN BEANS, CUT INTO
2.5 CM/1 IN LENGTHS

1 GREEN CHILLI, VERY FINELY
CHOPPED

175 ML/6 FL OZ COCONUT MILK

450 G/1 LB TOMATOES, SEEDED,
SKINNED AND CHOPPED

SALT AND GROUND BLACK PEPPER

100 G/4 OZ CASHEW NUTS, TOASTED

RICE, TO SERVE

CORIANDER SPRIG, TO GARNISH

NATURAL YOGHURT, TO SERVE

2 Cook the potatoes for 5 minutes, drain and cut into cubes. Add to the spices along with the remaining vegetables and chilli. Fry for 7-10 minutes, stirring occasionally.

3 Stir in the coconut milk and the tomatoes. Season, then simmer for 15-20 minutes.

4 Stir the cashews into the curry and then arrange on a bed of rice. Garnish with a coriander sprig, serve with a bowl of natural yoghurt.

1 Heat the oil in a heavy-based pan. Fry the crushed garlic, spices and chopped ginger for 3-4 minutes until soft but not brown.

TIP

THIS VEGETABLE CURRY CAN BE MADE uP TO 2 DAYS IN ADVANCE AND KEPT COVERED IN THE FRIDGE. ADD THE CASHEW NUTS ONCE THE CURRY IS REHEATED AND JUST BEFORE SERVING.

VEGETARIAN TACOS

Clint Brown

High in protein and fibre, low in calories and
fat, textured soya is an extremely healthy
alternative to meat. In this recipe, mixed with
spices, it tastes remarkably good – and
very Mexican!

PREPARATION TIME: 10 MINS
COOKING TIME: 1 HOUR 10 MINS
SERVES 4

I N G R E D I E N T S

100 G/4 OZ MINCED TEXTURED SOYA
PROTEIN (NATURAL FLAVOUR)

1 TBLS OIL

1 ONION, CHOPPED

2 CLOVES OF GARLIC, CHOPPED

400 G/14 OZ TINNED CHOPPED
TOMATOES

2 TBLS TOMATO PUREE

75 G/3 OZ RAISINS

2 TBLS RED WINE VINEGAR

1-2 TSP CHILLI POWDER

1 TSP GROUND CINNAMON

1 TSP GROUND CUMIN

1 TSP SUGAR

PINCH OF GROUND CLOVES

SALT AND GROUND BLACK PEPPER

8 TACO SHELLS

FOR THE TOPPING

¼ SHREDDED ICEBERG LETTUCE

100 G/4 OZ CHEDDAR CHEESE, GRATED

2 TINNED RED PIMIENTOS,
THINLY SLICED

8 STONED BLACK OLIVES, CHOPPED

the dried soya. Bring to the boil then simmer for 2 minutes. Remove from heat. Set aside

2 Heat the oil in a large frying-pan and fry the onion and garlic for 5 minutes until slightly softened. Add the tinned tomatoes, mince, tomato purée, raisins, vinegar, chilli powder, cinnamon, cumin, sugar and a pinch of ground cloves. Season with salt and ground black pepper to taste and stir thoroughly to mix. Cover and cook very gently for 1 hour. Preheat the oven to 180 C/350 F/Gas 4.

3 When the filling is cooked place the taco shells on a baking tray and heat in the oven for 2-3 minutes. Spoon the soya mixture into each shell. Top with shredded lettuce, cheese, pimientos and chopped olives.

1 First reconstitute the soya mince. Place 450 ml/¾ pt water in a saucepan, heat, then stir in

LENTIL LASAGNE

Michael Michaels

This wholewheat lasagne is a filling treat that's full of nutritious ingredients.

PREPARATION TIME: 15 MINS
COOKING TIME: 1 HOUR 18 MINS
SERVES 6

INGREDIENTS

350 G/12 OZ BROWN LENTILS

3 TBLS OLIVE OIL, PLUS EXTRA FOR
BRUSHING

1 LARGE ONION, CHOPPED

2 CLOVES OF GARLIC, CRUSHED

1 RED PEPPER, SEEDED AND
CHOPPED

100 G/4 OZ BUTTON MUSHROOMS,
CHOPPED

3 TBLS TOMATO PUREE

SALT AND GROUND BLACK PEPPER

3 TBLS CHOPPED FRESH THYME

2 TBLS DARK SOY SAUCE

150 ML/¼ PT VEGETABLE STOCK

3 TBLS RED WINE

6 SHEETS OF NO-NEED-TO-COOK
WHOLEWHEAT LASAGNE

100 G/4 OZ CHEDDAR, GRATED

2 BEEFSTEAK TOMATOES, SLICED

FOR THE TOPPING

2 BEATEN EGGS

300 ML/½ PT GREEK YOGHURT

PINCH OF NUTMEG

100 G/4 OZ CHEDDAR, GRATED

2 Preheat the oven to 190 C/375 F/ Gas 5. Heat the oil in a frying-pan. Fry the onion and garlic and stir until softened. Add the chopped red pepper and mushrooms and cook for 3-4 minutes over a moderate heat. Then add the lentils, tomato purée, seasoning, chopped thyme, soy sauce, vegetable stock and red wine. Stir well to combine the ingredients. Cook for 5 minutes.

3 Brush a 1.7 L/3 pt lasagne dish with olive oil, then lay 2 sheets of the wholewheat lasagne on the base of the dish. Spoon half the lentil mixture over the pasta and sprinkle over the Cheddar. Lay the tomatoes over the cheese then add 2 more sheets of lasagne on top. Spoon over the remaining lentil mixture, sprinkle the remaining Cheddar over the top and lay the final 2 sheets of lasagne carefully.

1 Cover the lentils with cold water. Bring to the boil and cook for 30-35 minutes or until soft. Drain.

4 Mix together the topping ingredients, reserving a little Cheddar and pour it over the lasagne. Sprinkle with the reserved Cheddar and bake for 30-35 minutes, until cooked and golden on the surface.

GALETTE

Hilary Moore

A savoury French cake made of layers of
vegetable purées and pancakes.

PREPARATION TIME: 10 MINS
COOKING TIME: 1 HOUR
SERVES 4-6

I N G R E D I E N T S

7 X 18 CM/7 IN PANCAKES
(SEE RECIPE PAGE 63)

2 TBLS PARMESAN, GRATED

BUTTER, FOR GREASING

FRESH BASIL, TO GARNISH

FOR THE FENNEL FILLING

450 G/1 LB FENNEL, SLICED

25 G/1 OZ BUTTER

50 G/2 OZ PARMESAN, GRATED

SALT AND GROUND BLACK PEPPER

FOR THE SPINACH FILLING

2 TBLS OLIVE OIL

1 SMALL ONION, FINELY CHOPPED

1 CLOVE OF GARLIC, CRUSHED

225 G/8 OZ FROZEN CHOPPED LEAF
SPINACH, THAWED AND DRAINED

½ TSP GRATED NUTMEG

GROUND BLACK PEPPER

FOR THE TOMATO FILLING

1 ONION, CHOPPED

1 CLOVE OF GARLIC, CRUSHED

2 TBLS OLIVE OIL

450 G/1 LB TOMATOES, SKINNED,
SEEDED AND CHOPPED

3 STICKS OF CELERY, CHOPPED

2 TBLS CHOPPED FRESH BASIL

1 TBLS TOMATO PUREE

1 Make the fennel filling: blanch the fennel for 5 minutes in boiling water. Drain well. Melt the butter in a pan and add the fennel. Cook, covered for 5 minutes until softened. Purée, then add the Parmesan and seasoning. Set aside. If too moist return to the pan before adding the cheese and cook, stirring, until moisture has evaporated.

2 Preheat the oven to 180 C/350 F/ Gas 4. Then make the spinach filling: heat the oil in a frying-pan. Add the onion and garlic and fry until softened. Add the spinach, nutmeg and pepper and cook for 5-8 minutes, then set aside until ready to use.

3 Finally make the tomato filling: gently fry the onion and garlic for 3-4 minutes in the oil. Stir in the tomatoes, celery, basil, tomato purée and seasoning. Cook, covered, for 10-15 minutes until a thick and creamy sauce is achieved. Set aside.

4 To assemble the galette lightly grease an 18 cm/7 in spring-form tin. Lay a pancake in the base of the tin, then spoon alternate fillings between the pancakes, reserving some tomato sauce. Finish the layering with a pancake. Sprinkle 1 tbls Parmesan on top and bake for 15-20 minutes. Remove from the tin and serve with reserved tomato sauce, and the rest of the Parmesan and garnish with fresh basil.

EASTER PIE

Peter Reilly

This delicious pie filled with ricotta cheese,
spinach and artichokes may be eaten
at any time of the year.

46

PREPARATION TIME: 50 MINS

COOKING TIME: 1 HOUR

SERVES 6

I N G R E D I E N T S

450 G/1 LB FLOUR
½ TSP SALT
3 TBLS OLIVE OIL, PLUS EXTRA FOR LAYERING
FOR THE FILLING
350 G/12 OZ CHOPPED FROZEN SPINACH, THAWED
350 G/12 OZ RICOTTA CHEESE
1 TBLS GRATED PARMESAN CHEESE
2 TBLS OLIVE OIL
7 EGGS
1 TBLS FRESH MARJORAM
SALT AND GROUND BLACK PEPPER
PINCH OF NUTMEG
400 G/14 OZ TINNED ARTICHOKE HEARTS, DRAINED
FLAT-LEAVED PARSLEY, TO GARNISH

1 To prepare the pastry, sieve the flour and salt into a bowl. Add 3 tbls of olive oil and 150 ml/¼ pt water and stir until it forms a soft dough. Cover and chill.

2 Squeeze out as much liquid as possible from the thawed spinach. Place in a mixing bowl with the ricotta and Parmesan cheeses and olive oil. Beat in two of the eggs with the marjoram. Season with salt, pepper and nutmeg and heat together until combined. Quarter the artichoke hearts and fold in.

3 Lightly grease a 20 cm/8 in loose-bottomed cake tin with olive oil and preheat the oven to 190 C/375 F/Gas 5. Divide the pastry in half and roll out one half large enough to line the tin, but do not trim the pastry edges. Divide remaining pastry in four and roll each into a 20 cm/8 in circle. Brush each layer with oil and sandwich one on top of the other.

Michael Michaels

4 To assemble the pie, spoon the filling into the pastry-lined tin and make four indentations. Break one egg into each recess. Cover with layered pastry circle and trim off excess pastry with a knife. Decorate the top with attractive pastry shapes made from the trimmings. Beat the remaining egg and glaze the pie. Bake in the centre of the oven for 1 hour. Allow to cool before turning out and garnishing.

CAMEMBERT & BROCCOLI ROULADE

Creamy, cheesy and tasty – serve this broccoli flavoured soufflé roll, filled with a Camembert sauce, as a hot savoury main course.

Michael Michaels

PREPARATION TIME: 15 MINS
COOKING TIME: 30 MINS
SERVES 6

I N G R E D I E N T S

25 G/1 OZ BUTTER, PLUS EXTRA FOR GREASING

6 TBLS PARMESAN CHEESE

575 G/1 LB 4 OZ BROCCOLI FLORETS

300 ML/1/2 PT VEGETABLE STOCK

2 TBLS GREEK STRAINED YOGHURT

4 EGGS, SEPARATED

PINCH OF GRATED NUTMEG

SALT AND GROUND BLACK PEPPER

FOR THE FILLING

25 G/1 OZ BUTTER

25 G/1 OZ FLOUR

200 ML/7 FL OZ MILK

1/2 A CAMEMBERT CHEESE, SKIN REMOVED

75 G/3 OZ PUMPKIN SEEDS

SALAD, TO SERVE

1 Preheat the oven to 190 C/375 F/ Gas 5. Grease and line a 25-33 cm/10-13 in Swiss roll tin with baking parchment, then sprinkle with 3 tbls Parmesan cheese. Cook broccoli in stock until tender. Drain. Reserve 5 florets for garnish, roughly chop the rest.

2 Melt the butter in a pan and gently sauté the chopped broccoli. Stir in the yoghurt. Remove the pan from the heat and add the egg yolks, beating thoroughly. Whisk the egg whites until stiff but not dry and fold them into the broccoli. Add the nutmeg and season with salt and pepper. Spoon into the prepared tin and bake for 15-20 minutes until it becomes puffy and set.

3 Meanwhile, prepare the filling: Melt the butter in a saucepan and stir in the flour. Blend well and gradually add the milk.

4 Return the pan to the heat and bring to the boil, stirring continuously. Add the Camembert cheese. Remove from the heat. Stir in the pumpkin seeds. Dampen a clean tea-towel with water and cover with a large piece of greaseproof paper. Sprinkle with the remaining 3 tbls Parmesan cheese.

5 Turn the roulade out onto the greaseproof paper and carefully peel off the lining paper. Spread the roulade with the cheese filling and roll up, using the tea-towel to help. Garnish and serve immediately with the salad.

ASPARAGUS & ALMONDS IN FILO

Clint Brown

A luxury dish that should win converts from the meat-and-two-veg brigade.

PREPARATION TIME: 15 MINS
COOKING TIME: 40 MINS
SERVES 4-6

I N G R E D I E N T S

5 SHEETS OF FILO PASTRY, THAWED
IF FROZEN

100 G/4 OZ BUTTER, MELTED, PLUS
EXTRA FOR GREASING

FOR THE FILLING

25 G/1 OZ BUTTER

1 ONION, FINELY CHOPPED

450 G/1 LB FRESH ASPARAGUS
SPEARS, TRIMMED AND BLANCHED OR
450 G/1 LB FROZEN ASPARAGUS,
THAWED AND DRAINED

100 G/4 OZ FLAKED ALMONDS,
TOASTED

6 TBLS SINGLE CREAM

100 G/4 OZ MATURE CHEDDAR
CHEESE, GRATED

SALT AND GROUND BLACK PEPPER

3 Brush the first sheet of filo pastry with melted butter and cover with a second sheet. Brush with butter again and repeat the process three times.

4 Spread the filling over the filo pastry, leaving a 2.5 cm/1 in border around the edge. Fold in the 2 shorter sides then roll up.

1 To make the filling, melt 25 g/1 oz of the butter in a frying-pan and sauté the onion until softened. Cut the asparagus into 2.5 cm/1 in pieces and fry briefly with onions. Stir in the almonds, cream, cheese and seasoning to taste. Set aside to cool.

2 Preheat the oven to 200 C/400 F/ Gas 6. Lay one sheet of filo pastry out on a work surface. Cover the remaining sheets with a just-damp cloth.

5 Lift the filo roll onto a buttered baking tray. Brush the pastry thoroughly with remaining melted butter and cook for 20 minutes. Turn the oven down to 180 C/350 F/Gas 4 and cook for a further 10 minutes or until crisp.

 SERVE SLICED, EITHER HOT WITH JULIENNE VEGETABLES OR COLD WITH SALAD.

VEGETABLE CREAM PIE

Dave Gill

You can use almost any mixture of colourful fresh or frozen vegetables to layer with these three tasty sauces.

PREPARATION TIME: 15 MINS
COOKING TIME: 25 MINS
SERVES 6

INGREDIENTS

225 G/8 OZ FRESH LEAF SPINACH OR
A BUNCH OF WATERCRESS

3 LARGE RIPE TOMATOES

900 ML/1 1/2 PT THICK HOMEMADE
BECHAMEL MADE WITH 75G/3OZ
EACH OF BUTTER AND FLOUR
(SEE RECIPE PAGE 63)

100 G/4 OZ MATURE CHEDDAR,
GRATED

¼ TSP GRATED NUTMEG

900 G/2 LB MIXED FRESHLY COOKED
VEGETABLES (BROCCOLI, CARROTS,
SWEETCORN, PEAS, BEANS)

1 TBLS FRESH WHITE BREADCRUMBS

1 Cook the spinach or watercress leaves briefly in boiling water until wilted but still bright green. Drain and squeeze dry. Prick the tomato skins and leave in boiling water for a few seconds. Remove the skins and slice.

2 Divide the béchamel sauce into three. Add the spinach to one, 50 g/2 oz of the cheese to the second and the nutmeg to the third. Liquidise the spinach sauce.

SERVE THIS COLOURFUL PIE WITH BAKED POTATOES AND A CRISP GREEN SALAD.

3 Preheat the oven to 200 C/400 F/ Gas 6. Make layers of the vegetables and sauces in a large deep ovenproof dish – preferably a clear one so you can see the layers. Start with broccoli, tomatoes and white sauce, then add carrots and the green sauce, then sweetcorn, peas and beans, and finally pour over the cheese sauce.

4 Sprinkle over the remaining grated cheese and the breadcrumbs. Bake for 25 minutes or until the topping is lightly browned.

TIP

MAKE SURE THE VEGETABLES ARE DRAINED WELL BEFORE YOU LAYER THEM WITH THE SAUCES — EXCESS WATER WILL DILUTE THE BECHAMEL.

PEPPERS WITH LENTIL STUFFING

Alan Newnham

Yellow, white and orange peppers are now available along with the well-known red and green ones, so this can be a very colourful dish. The cool cream in the topping perfectly complements the spicy lentils.

PREPARATION TIME: 10 MINS
COOKING TIME: 45 MINS
SERVES 4

I N G R E D I E N T S

100 G/4 OZ RED LENTILS
50 G/2 OZ GHEE OR BUTTER
1 ONION, CHOPPED
1 CLOVE OF GARLIC, CRUSHED
1 COOKING APPLE, PEELED AND DICED
50 G/2 OZ STONED DATES, CHOPPED
1 TBLS GROUND CORIANDER
2 TSP GROUND CUMIN
SALT AND GROUND BLACK PEPPER
4 PLUMP PEPPERS
FOR THE TOPPING
2 GREEN OR RED CHILLIES
1 TBLS OIL
150 ML/¼ PT SOURED CREAM

1 Preheat the oven to 190 C/375 F/ Gas 5. Place the lentils in a saucepan and add sufficient water to cover the lentils by at least 2.5 cm/ 1 in. Bring to the boil, reduce the heat and cover. Simmer for 6-7 minutes or until tender then drain thoroughly.

2 Melt the ghee or butter in a frying-pan, add the onion and garlic and cook gently for about 3 minutes until soft. Add the apple and

dates and cook, stirring for 2-3 minutes then remove from the heat. Stir in the drained lentils, coriander, cumin, salt and pepper and cook for 1 minute.

Peter Reilly

3 Halve the peppers lengthways and cut out the cores and seeds. Place in a roasting tin. Spoon the lentil mixture into the pepper halves. Cover the dish with foil and bake in the centre of the oven for 25-30 minutes or until the peppers are tender.

4 While the peppers are cooking, make the topping. Cut out the stalks from the chillies and then remove the cores and seeds. Rinse to remove any extra seeds and slice into thin rings. Heat the oil in a small frying-pan, add the chillies and fry for 30 seconds until bright green or red. Remove with a slotted spoon and drain.

5 Arrange the cooked peppers on a large heated serving dish. Spoon the soured cream over the top, sprinkle with the chilli rings and serve.

 THE LENTIL STUFFING CAN BE MADE IN ADVANCE. COVER AND FREEZE FOR UP TO 6 MONTHS.

GARLIC AUBERGINES

Hillary Moore

<u>Make this dish with good quality olive oil
for maximum flavour and good health.</u>

PREPARATION TIME: 25 MINS
+ STANDING
COOKING TIME: 1 HOUR 5 MINS
SERVES 8

I N G R E D I E N T S

| 8 AUBERGINES |
| SALT AND GROUND BLACK PEPPER |
| 450 G/1 LB ONIONS, SLICED |
| 200 ML/7 FL OZ OLIVE OIL |
| 4 CLOVES OF GARLIC, CRUSHED |
| 4 TBLS FINELY CHOPPED FRESH PARSLEY |
| 450 G/1 LB RIPE TOMATOES |
| 1½ TSP SUGAR |
| JUICE OF 1 LARGE LEMON |
| SPRIGS OF PARSLEY, TO GARNISH |
| TOMATO SLICES, TO GARNISH |

alternate stripes of peeled and unpeeled flesh. Make a lengthways slit right down the aubergine. Sprinkle the inside and out heavily with salt and leave to stand for 1 hour to extract some of the juices.

3 Preheat the oven to 190 C/375 F/ Gas 5. Rinse the aubergines, dry and scoop out the flesh. Keep the shell intact. Chop the flesh.

4 Gently fry the onions in 3 tbls of the oil until soft. Add the aubergine flesh. Stir for 30 seconds, then add the garlic and chopped parsley. Skin, seed and chop the tomatoes and add to the pan. Season. Mix then spoon into the aubergines.

1 Pull the leaves from the stalk end of the aubergines, but leave 12 mm/½ in of the stalk attached.

5 Pack the aubergines, split side up in a roasting tin and cover with the remaining olive oil. Sprinkle with the sugar and pepper to taste. Add 150 ml/¼ pt water. Sprinkle with the lemon juice. Cover and cook in the oven for 1 hour or until very soft. Leave the stuffed aubergines to cool until they are lukewarm, then carefully transfer onto a serving dish. Garnish with sprigs of fresh parsley and sliced tomato.

2 Peel strips of skin lengthways with a potato peeler down the aubergine, leaving narrow

BAKED ARTICHOKES

Paul Moon

For a true taste of the Mediterranean try these baked artichokes filled with aromatic herbs and seasonings. Simply serve with crusty bread to mop up the juices . . . delicious!

PREPARATION TIME: 40 MINS
COOKING TIME: 1 HOUR
SERVES 4

I N G R E D I E N T S

4 ARTICHOKES

JUICE AND ZEST OF 2 LEMONS

1 CLOVE OF GARLIC, SLICED

4 SPRIGS FLAT-LEAVED PARSLEY

4 SPRIGS OF FRESH MINT

125 ML/4 FL OZ OLIVE OIL

SALT AND GROUND BLACK PEPPER

SPRIG OF BASIL, TO GARNISH

FOR THE STUFFING

1 RED PEPPER, FINELY CHOPPED

2 TBLS CAPERS, DRAINED AND
CHOPPED

6 TBLS FRESH WHOLEMEAL
BREADCRUMBS

3 TBLS FRESH CHOPPED PARSLEY

10 LARGE BASIL LEAVES, CHOPPED

1 CLOVE OF GARLIC, CRUSHED

3 TBLS OLIVE OIL

2 When you reach the mauve-coloured choke, pull out and discard. Use a spoon to remove all the hair at the bottom. Continue the procedure with each artichoke. As each one is prepared, place in a bowl of cold water with the lemon juice. This helps prevent the artichokes discolouring or drying out before they are stuffed.

3 Preheat the oven to 190 C/375 F/ Gas 5. For the stuffing: combine all the stuffing ingredients and mix well. Drain the artichokes, then spoon the stuffing into the middles and place upside-down in a deep baking dish or casserole. Add lemon zest, garlic, parsley, mint and 50 ml/2 fl oz of water to the dish. Pour over the olive oil and season with salt and black pepper.

1 Cut the ends of the stems off the artichokes. Then, using a sharp knife, scrape each stem to remove the tough outer skin. Carefully tear the dark green leaves off, leaving the fleshy bottom parts of the artichoke intact. Continue down the artichoke until the leaves are just green at the very tip. Cut the tips off with scissors.

4 Cover the dish tightly with foil or a tight lid. Bake for 50-60 minutes until the artichokes are tender when pierced with a sharp knife. Garnish with basil and serve with the juice.

VEGETABLE STUFFED MARROW

Nick Carman

Marrow with a difference, served cut across into slices and filled with a distinct Middle Eastern-flavoured stuffing.

PREPARATION TIME: 40 MINS
+ SOAKING
COOKING TIME: 40 MINS
SERVES 4-6

INGREDIENTS

15 G/½ OZ COUSCOUS

25 G/1 OZ BUTTER, PLUS EXTRA FOR
GREASING

2 CLOVES OF GARLIC, CRUSHED

1 LEEK, THINLY SLICED

50 G/2 OZ MUSHROOMS, SLICED

50 G/2 OZ ADZUKI BEANS, SOAKED
OVERNIGHT AND COOKED

2 TSP PARSLEY, CHOPPED

1 TBLS THYME, CHOPPED

1 LARGE MARROW

FLAT-LEAVED PARSLEY, TO GARNISH

FOR THE SAUCE

25 G/1 OZ BUTTER

4 SPRING ONIONS, SLICED

25 G/1 OZ FLOUR

300 ML/½ PT MILK

50 G/2 OZ RED LEICESTER CHEESE

1 SPRING ONION, CHOPPED

2 Grease a roasting tin. Slice the marrow and remove and discard the centres. Fill with stuffing, place in the tin and add 125 ml/4 fl oz water. Cover the tin and bake the marrow in the oven for 30 minutes.

1 Soak the couscous for 30 minutes then drain. Preheat the oven to 190 C/375 F/Gas 5. Melt the butter in a pan and sauté the garlic and leek for 1 minute. Add the mushrooms and sauté for a further minute. Stir in the beans, herbs and couscous. Set aside.

3 To make the sauce, melt the butter and sauté the onions for 2 minutes. Stir in the flour and gradually stir in the milk, off the heat. Return the pan to the heat and cook, stirring until the sauce thickens. Grate cheese, stir in and heat gently to melt.

4 Spoon the sauce over the bases of serving plates. Drain the marrow well. Put a slice of marrow onto each plate, sprinkle onion around the marrow and garnish with parsley.

TIP

LOOK FOR A RIPE MARROW – THIS SHOULD BE FIRM AND FEEL HEAVY. STORE IN A COOL DRY PLACE FOR UP TO 3 DAYS.

BASIC RECIPES

RICH SHORTCRUST PASTRY

Rich shortcrust pastry is basically a shortcrust pastry mixture made with butter plus an egg yolk. Make sure everything is nice and cool and don't overwork the mixture. Rinse your hands in cold water before you start and chill the made-up dough before cooking. The made-up pastry can be stored in the fridge for 3 to 4 days. Use this pastry for flans and double-crust pies. Use wholemeal flour instead of plain for a darker pastry.

PREPARATION TIME: 10 MINS + CHILLING
MAKES ABOUT 350 G/12 OZ RICH SHORTCRUST PASTRY

INGREDIENTS

225 G/8 OZ FLOUR
PINCH OF SALT
115 G/4½ OZ BUTTER
1 EGG YOLK
2 TBLS CHILLED WATER

1 Sift the flour and salt into a bowl and rub in the butter. Mix the egg yolk with the chilled water and add to the mixture.

2 Mix to a firm dough – first by mixing with a round-ended knife and then finishing off with one hand. You may need to add more water, but go easy here: the pastry shouldn't be too damp as this will produce a tougher texture. Wrap the pastry in cling film and chill and relax for 30 minutes.

TOMATO SAUCE

This fresh-tasting tomato sauce is a world away from the ready-made kind that comes in bottles.

PREPARATION TIME: 10 MINS
COOKING TIME: 30 MINS
MAKES 300 ML/½ PT

INGREDIENTS

400 G/14 OZ TINNED TOMATOES
1 SMALL ONION, CHOPPED
1 CARROT, CHOPPED
1 STICK OF CELERY, CHOPPED
½ A CLOVE OF GARLIC, CRUSHED
1 BAY LEAF
2-3 FRESH PARSLEY STALKS
SALT AND GROUND BLACK PEPPER
JUICE OF ½ A LEMON
DASH OF WORCESTERSHIRE SAUCE
1 TSP SUGAR
1 TSP FRESHLY CHOPPED BASIL
TO SERVE
CONTINENTAL SAUSAGES
MASHED POTATOES

1 Put all the ingredients in a heavy-based pan and simmer over medium heat for 30 minutes.

2 Strain the sauce through a sieve and return it to the pan. It should coat and cling to the back of a spoon. If the sauce is too thin, reduce by boiling rapidly. Check the seasoning. Serve with garlicky continental sausages and mashed potatoes.

PANCAKES

PREPARATION TIME: 5 MINS
COOKING TIME: 30 MINS
MAKES 450 ML/3/4 PT

INGREDIENTS

100 G/4 OZ FLOUR

PINCH OF SALT

1 LARGE EGG

1 EGG YOLK

300 ML/½ PT MILK

1 TBLS OIL

1 Sieve the flour and salt together into a large bowl and make a well in the centre of the flour.

2 Into this well, break the egg then add the egg yolk and pour in a little of the milk.

3 Using a whisk, mix the egg and milk together and then gradually draw in the flour from the sides as you beat in more milk until you have a batter which is the consistency of half-whipped cream. Beat the batter until smooth then stir in the oil.

4 Continue to beat in the remaining milk – the batter should now be the consistency of thin cream. Cover the bowl and set the batter aside for 30 minutes – this will give the cooked batter more lightness.

5 Heat a frying pan, wipe around with a little oil and then pour in 25 ml/1 fl oz batter. Swirl the pan around and cook for one minute. Flip the pancake and cook the other side until golden brown. Repeat the process with the remaining batter.

BECHAMEL SAUCE

Béchamel is the French version of white sauce. The milk is infused with onion, mace, peppercorns, bay leaf and parsley.

PREPARATION TIME: 10 MINS
COOKING TIME: 10 MINS
MAKES 300 ML/½ PT

INGREDIENTS

300 ML/½ PT MILK

SLICE OF ONION

BLADE OF MACE

FEW FRESH PARSLEY STALKS

4 PEPPERCORNS

1 BAY LEAF

20 G/¾ OZ BUTTER

20 G/¾ OZ FLOUR

1 TBLS CREAM

SALT AND GROUND WHITE PEPPER

1 Place the milk with the onion, mace, parsley, peppercorns and bay leaf in a saucepan and slowly bring to simmering point.

2 Reduce the heat and allow the flavour to infuse for about 8-10 minutes. Strain.

3 Make a white roux: melt the butter in a thick-based saucepan, stir in the flour and cook, stirring, over moderate heat for 1 minute.

4 Remove from the heat. Gradually whisk the infused milk into the roux, a little at a time, adding more milk when the last addition is thoroughly mixed in. Return the sauce to the heat and stir or whisk until boiling. Simmer for 2-3 minutes and add the cream. Taste and season.

INDEX

PANCAKES & TACOS
Galette 44
Pancakes 63
Vegetarian Tacos 40

PASTA
Lentil Lasagne 42
Pepper Tomato Sauce with Pasta 28
Saffron Pasta with Pimientos 30
Stuffed Tomatoes 18
Tagliatelle with Mushroom Sauce 26

PIES & BREADS
Asparagus & Almonds in Filo 50
Easter Pie 46
Galette 44
Rich Shortcrust Pastry 62
Roquefort & Leek Tartlets 6
Vegetable Cream Pie 52
Vegetable Croustade 32

ROULADES & MOUSSES
Camembert & Broccoli Roulade 48
Mixed Vegetable Mousses 4

STEWS & SAUCES
Bechamel Sauce 63
Braised Chicory with Apple 22
Celeriac Gratin 20
Ratatouille 24
Tomato Sauce 62
Wild Mushrooms in Basil Sauce 8

STIR-FRIES & CURRIES
Chinese Vegetable Stir-Fry 36
Sweet & Sour Vegetables 34
Vegetable & Cashew Curry 38

STUFFED VEGETABLES
Baked Artichokes 58
Cream Stuffed Kohlrabi 14
Garlic Aubergines 56
Peppers with Lentil Stuffing 54
Stuffed Tomatoes 18
Vegetable Stuffed Marrow 60

TERRINES & SOUFFLES
Layered Vegetable Terrine 10
Leek Terrine 12
Souffle Avocados 16